I0391049

Draw It!
By Lawson Co.

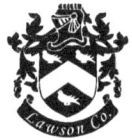

Life is about making an impact, not making an income.
- Kevin Kruse

It is a good thing for an uneducated man to read books of quotations
- Winston Churchill

Strive not to be a success, but rather to be of value.
- Albert Einstein

There are a terrible lot of lies going about the world, and the worst of it is that half of them are true. - Winston Churchill

I attribute my success to this:
I never gave or took any excuse. –Florence Nightingale

To build may have to be the slow and laborious task of years.
To destroy can be the thoughtless act of a single day. - Winston Churchill

The most difficult thing is the decision to act, the rest is merely tenacity.
–Amelia Earhart

To improve is to change, so to be perfect is to change often.
- Winston Churchill

The farther backward you can look, the farther forward you are likely to see.
- Winston Churchill

Life isn't about getting and having, it's about giving and being.
- Kevin Kruse

> *Life is what happens to you while you're busy making other plans.*
> *- John Lennon*

We become what we think about. - Earl Nightingale

Life is 10% what happens to me and 90% of how I react to it.
- Charles Swindoll

The most common way people give up their power is by thinking they don't have any. - Alice Walker

The mind is everything. What you think you become. *- Buddha*

The best time to plant a tree was 20 years ago. The second best time is now. - Chinese Proverb

An unexamined life is not worth living. - Socrates

Eighty percent of success is showing up. - Woody Allen

The price of greatness is responsibility. - Winston Churchill

Winning isn't everything, but wanting to win is. - Vince Lombardi

> *I am not a product of my circumstances.*
> *I am a product of my decisions. - Stephen Covey*

Every child is an artist.
The problem is how to remain an artist once he grows up. - Pablo Picasso

Men occasionally stumble over the truth, but most of them pick themselves up and hurry off as if nothing ever happened. - Winston Churchill

I've learned that people will forget what you said, people will forget what you did, but people will never forget how you made them feel. - Maya Angelou

Either you run the day, or the day runs you. - Jim Rohn

Whether you think you can or you think you can't, you're right.
- Henry Ford

The two most important days in your life are the day you are born and the day you find out why. - Mark Twain

Whatever you can do, or dream you can, begin it.
Boldness has genius, power and magic in it. - Johann Wolfgang von Goethe

*Never hold discussions with the monkey when the organ
grinder is in the room. - Winston Churchill*

People often say that motivation doesn't last. Well, neither does bathing. That's why we recommend it daily. - Zig Ziglar

If you hear a voice within you say "you cannot paint," then by all means paint and that voice will be silenced. - Vincent Van Gogh

Success is the ability to go from one failure to another with no loss of enthusiasm. - Winston Churchill

Ask and it will be given to you; search, and you will find;
knock and the door will be opened for you. - Jesus

The only person you are destined to become is the person you decide to be.
- Ralph Waldo Emerson

Go confidently in the direction of your dreams.
Live the life you have imagined. - Henry David Thoreau

Few things can help an individual more than to place responsibility on him, and to let him know that you trust him. - Booker T. Washington

Certain things catch your eye, but pursue only those that capture the heart. - Ancient Indian Proverb

Believe you can and you're halfway there.
- Theodore Roosevelt

Everything you've ever wanted is on the other side of fear.
- George Addair

*Broadly speaking short words are best and the old words when short,
are best of all. - Winston Churchill*

> *Courage is rightly esteemed the first of human qualities because it has been said, it is the quality which guarantees all others.*
> *- Winston Churchill*

Start where you are. Use what you have. Do what you can.
- Arthur Ashe

Fall seven times and stand up eight. - Japanese Proverb

When one door of happiness closes, another opens,
but often we look so long at the closed door that we do not see
the one that has been opened for us. - Helen Keller

Everything has beauty,
but not everyone can see. - Confucius

How wonderful it is that nobody need wait a single moment before starting to improve the world. - Anne Frank

When I let go of what I am, I become what I might be.
- Lao Tzu

History will be kind to me for I intend to write it.
- Winston Churchill

Happiness is not something readymade.
It comes from your own actions. - Dalai Lama

If you're offered a seat on a rocket ship,
don't ask what seat! Just get on. - Sheryl Sandberg

First, have a definite, clear practical ideal; a goal, an objective. Second, have the necessary means to achieve your ends; wisdom, money, materials, and methods. Third, adjust all your means to that end. - Aristotle

If the wind will not serve, take to the oars. - Latin Proverb

You can't fall if you don't climb.
But there's no joy in living your whole life on the ground. - Unknown

Attitude is a little thing that makes a BIG difference. - Winston Churchill

Too many of us are not living our dreams because we are living our fears.
- Les Brown

If you want to lift yourself up, lift up someone else.
- Booker T. Washington

I have been impressed with the urgency of doing. Knowing is not enough; we must apply. Being willing is not enough; we must do. - Leonardo da Vinci

If you're going through hell, keep going. - Winston Churchill

Everyone has his day, and some days last longer than others.
- Winston Churchill

What's money? A man is a success if he gets up in the morning and goes to bed at night and in between does what he wants to do. - Bob Dylan

I didn't fail the test. I just found 100 ways to do it wrong.
- Benjamin Franklin

*In order to succeed, your desire for success should
be greater than your fear of failure. - Bill Cosby*

Politics is the ability to foretell what is going to happen tomorrow, next week, next month and next year. And to have the ability afterwards to explain why it didn't happen.
- Winston Churchill

There are no traffic jams along the extra mile. - Roger Staubach

It is never too late to be what you might have been. - George Eliot

You become what you believe. - Oprah Winfrey

> *I would rather die of passion than of boredom.*
> *- Vincent van Gogh*

A truly rich man is one whose children run into his arms when his hands are empty. - Unknown

> *It is not what you do for your children, but what you have taught them to do for themselves, that will make them successful human beings.*
> *- Ann Landers*

If you want your children to turn out well, spend twice as much time with them, and half as much money. - Abigail Van Buren

Build your own dreams, or someone else will hire you to build theirs. - Farrah Gray

Those who can win a war well can rarely make a good peace,
and those who could make a good peace would never have won the war.
- Winston Churchill

I have learned over the years that when one's mind is made up,
this diminishes fear. - Rosa Parks

> *It does not matter how slowly you go as long as you do not stop.*
> *- Confucius*

If you look at what you have in life, you'll always have more.
If you look at what you don't have in life, you'll never have enough.
- Oprah Winfrey

Remember that not getting what you want is sometimes
a wonderful stroke of luck. - Dalai Lama

You can't use up creativity. The more you use, the more you have.
- Maya Angelou

Dream big and dare to fail. - Norman Vaughan

Our lives begin to end the day we become silent about things that matter.
- Martin Luther King Jr.

Do what you can, where you are, with what you have.
- Teddy Roosevelt

If you do what you've always done, you'll get what you've always gotten.
- Tony Robbins

Dreaming, after all, is a form of planning. - Gloria Steinem

It's your place in the world; it's your life. Go on and do all you can with it, and make it the life you want to live. - Mae Jemison

You may be disappointed if you fail, but you are doomed if you don't try.
- Beverly Sills

Remember no one can make you feel inferior without your consent.
- Eleanor Roosevelt

We shape our dwellings, and afterwards our dwellings shape us.
- Winston Churchill

The question isn't who is going to let me; it's who is going to stop me.
- Ayn Rand

When everything seems to be going against you,
remember that the airplane takes off against the wind, not with it.
- Henry Ford

It's not the years in your life that count. It's the life in your years.
- Abraham Lincoln

Change your thoughts and you change your world.
- Norman Vincent Peale

What is adequacy? Adequacy is no standard at all.
- Winston Churchill

Nothing is impossible, the word itself says, "I'm possible!"
- Audrey Hepburn

There is always much to be said for not attempting more than you can do and for making a certainty of what you try. But this principle, like others in life and war, has it exceptions. - Winston Churchill

If you can dream it, you can achieve it. - Zig Ziglar

It is a good thing for an uneducated man to read books of quotations
- Winston Churchill

> *There are a terrible lot of lies going about the world, and the worst of it is that half of them are true. - Winston Churchill*

There is only one duty, only one safe course, and that is to try to be right and not to fear to do or say what you believe to be right. - Winston Churchill

In the course of my life I have often had to eat my words, and I must confess that I have always found it a wholesome diet. - Winston Churchill

Two roads diverged in a wood, and I—I took the one less traveled by,
And that has made all the difference.   - Robert Frost

> *Life is what we make it, always has been, always will be.*
> *- Grandma Moses*

Every man should ask himself each day whether he is not too readily accepting negative solutions. - Winston Churchill

You can never cross the ocean until you have the courage to lose sight of the shore. - Christopher Columbus

It is wonderful what great strides can be made when there is a resolute purpose behind them. - Winston Churchill

The first duty of the university is to teach wisdom, not a trade; character, not technicalities. We want a lot of engineers in the modern world, but we do not want a world of engineers. - Winston Churchill

We must believe that we are gifted for something, and that this thing, at whatever cost, must be attained. - Marie Curie

In finance, everything that is agreeable is unsound and everything that is sound is disagreeable. - Winston Churchill

The only way to do great work is to love what you do.
- Steve Jobs

Whatever the mind of man can conceive and believe, it can achieve.
- Napoleon Hill

The greatest lesson in life is to know that even fools are right sometimes.
- Winston Churchill

You miss 100% of the shots you don't take. - Wayne Gretzky

Teach thy tongue to say, "I do not know," and thous shalt progress.
- Maimonides

All the greatest things are simple, and many can be expressed in a single word: freedom; justice; honour; duty; mercy; hope. - Winston Churchill

The whole history of the world is summed up in the fact that when nations are strong they are not always just, and when they wish to be just, they are often no longer strong. - Winston Churchill

*The person who says it cannot be done should not interrupt
the person who is doing it. - Chinese Proverb*

I like pigs. Dogs look up to us. Cats look down on us.
Pigs treat us as equals. - Winston Churchill

If we open a quarrel between the past and the present we shall find that we have lost the future. - Winston Churchill

Challenges are what make life interesting and overcoming them is what makes life meaningful. - Joshua J. Marine

It is a mistake to try to look too far ahead. The chain of destiny can only be grasped one link at a time. - Winston Churchill

A person who never made a mistake never tried anything new.
- Albert Einstein

It's not enough that we do our best;
sometimes we have to do what's required. - Winston Churchill

*Life is not measured by the number of breaths we take,
but by the moments that take our breath away. - Maya Angelou*

*Definiteness of purpose is the
starting point of all achievement. - W. Clement Stone*

The problems of victory are more agreeable than those of defeat,
but they are no less difficult. - Winston Churchill

When the eagles are silent,
the parrots begin to jabber. - Winston Churchill

*We can easily forgive a child who is afraid of the dark;
the real tragedy of life is when men are afraid of the light. - Plato*

The best revenge is massive success. - Frank Sinatra

Out of intense complexities,
intense simplicities emerge. - Winston Churchill

Courage is what it takes to stand up and speak,
it's also what it takes to sit down and listen. - Winston Churchill

Every strike brings me closer to the next home run. - Babe Ruth

Limitations live only in our minds. But if we use our imaginations,
our possibilities become limitless. - Jamie Paolinetti

Continuous effort – not strength or intelligence –
is the key to unlocking our potential. - Winston Churchill

The battles that count aren't the ones for gold medals. The struggles within your-self–the invisible battles inside all of us–that's where it's at. - Jesse Owens

The farther backward you can look,
the farther forward you are likely to see. - Winston Churchill

Either write something worth reading or
do something worth writing. - Benjamin Franklin

Life shrinks or expands in proportion to one's courage.
- Anais Nin

It is a good thing for an uneducated man to read books of quotations - Winston Churchill

There is only one way to avoid criticism:
do nothing, say nothing, and be nothing. - Aristotle

The price of greatness is responsibility.
- Winston Churchill

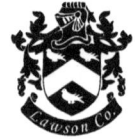

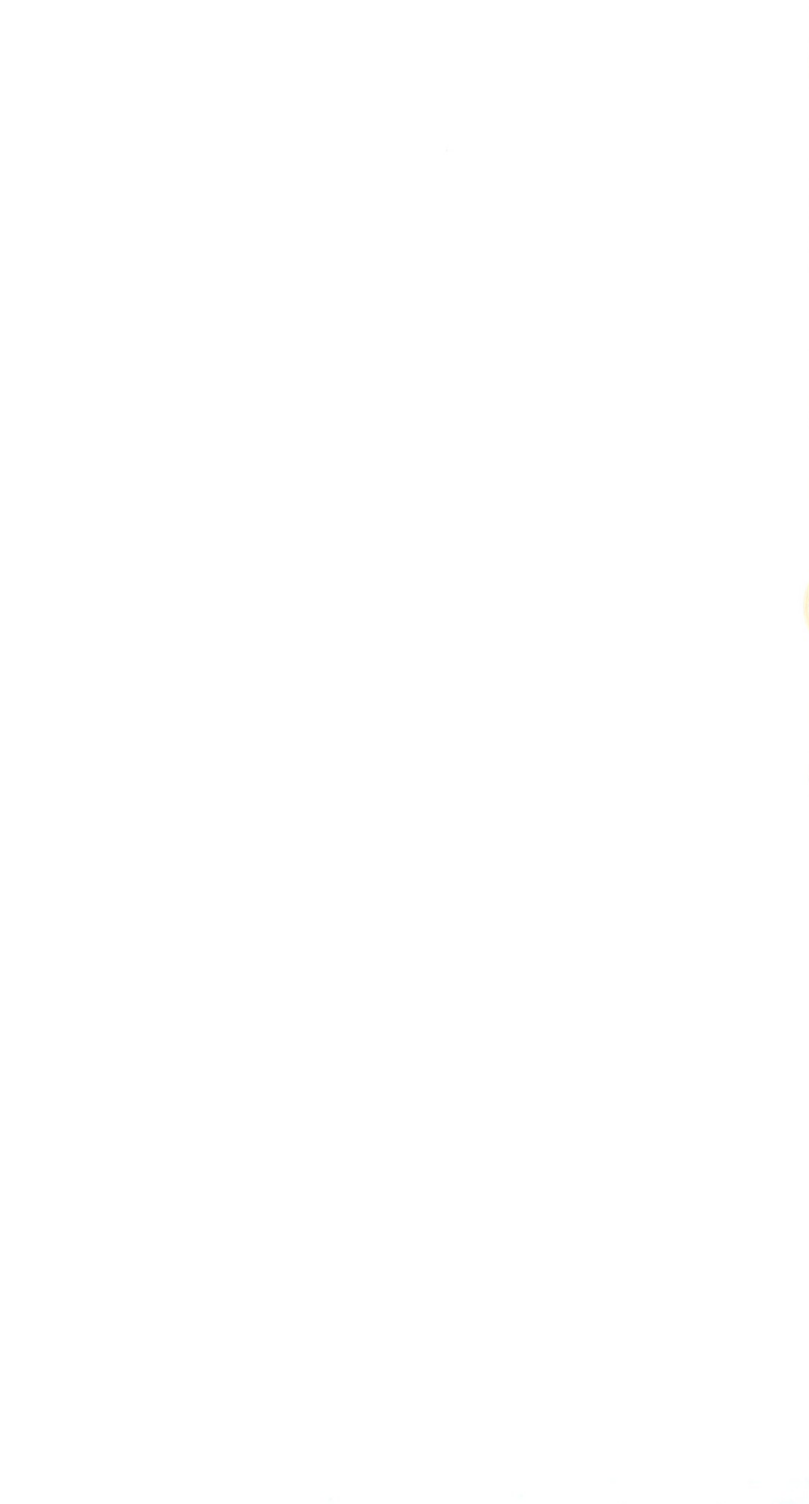

www.ingramcontent.com/pod-product-compliance
Lightning Source LLC
Chambersburg PA
CBHW061439180526
45170CB00004B/1472